New Seasons is a registered trademark of Publications International, Ltd.

Louis Weber, CEO
Publications International, Ltd.
7373 North Cicero Avenue
Lincolnwood, Illinois 60712

www.pilbooks.com

Manufactured in China.

8 7 6 5 4 3 2 1

ISBN-13: 978-1-4127-4050-0
ISBN-10: 1-4127-4050-9

If Dogs Could Talk

TONGUES UNLEASHED!

Written by Joel Zadak

new seasons®

No, because if I "drop it" you're just going to throw it again.

I'm only waiting tables until I get a callback from Animal Planet, which should be any day now.

I do love you. I'm just not ready to announce it to the world.

Wanna go outside? Let's go outside. Can we go outside? We should go outside. Have you been outside?

I don't care how much they paid for the couch. I slept on the old one and I'm sleeping on this one.

I won't tell
if you
won't tell.

The fresh paint tasted
soooo good.

Blondes do
have more
fun.

Right now I'm doing your typical puppy jobs, but what I really want is to direct.

I have to walk
her twice a day.

My backside smiles so much,
my mouth doesn't have to.

I'll hide out
here until
they put the
two-year-old
to bed.

I may not be able to run anymore, but I'm wise enough to appreciate the days when I could.

I know I messed up, but people really need to realize they can't have nice things _and_ a puppy.

Mrs. Johnson owns us all, so yeah, I guess that means we're related.

They
always say
they'll only
be a
minute.

I like the idea of a sandwich,
I just never had the patience
to actually make one.

Can we do a picture with just the two of us? My ribs are killing me.

We have to go home now.
I have to call my broker.

I ran. I got the ball.
I brought it back.
Now what?

I wasn't worried, until he started calling me his little McNugget.

Yeah, I ate the boy's homework. That's what I love to do, eat boys' homework.

Why do you guys think Mom's so happy all of a sudden?

No squirrel may pass. I am the
Squirrel Master.

Uh, you guys might want to sleep downstairs tonight.

Pssst . . .
do you want
to know a
secret?

Drop it. Drop it. Drop it.
Drop it. Come on, drop it.

This is torture. Someone call the ASPCA.

You're definitely
picking the
wrong day to
mess with me.

Come to think of it, I probably should have opted for the money-back guarantee.

Pardon me, but what does this sign say? I can't read.

Come on now,
big girls
don't cry.

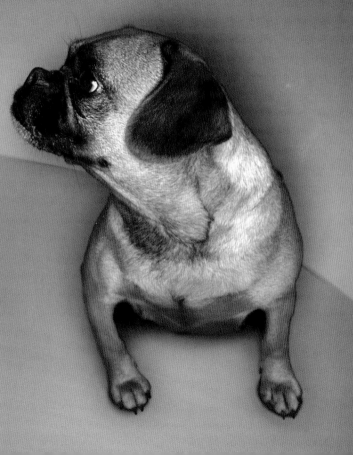

I can't believe we
have the same mother.

What obedience class? I was trained on the streets.

Sometimes I feel I'm a Jack
Russell trapped in a bulldog's
body. But then that goes away and
I just sleep the rest of the day.

The end.

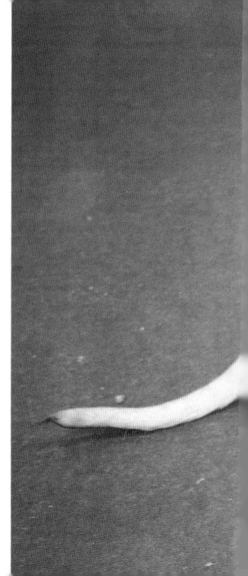

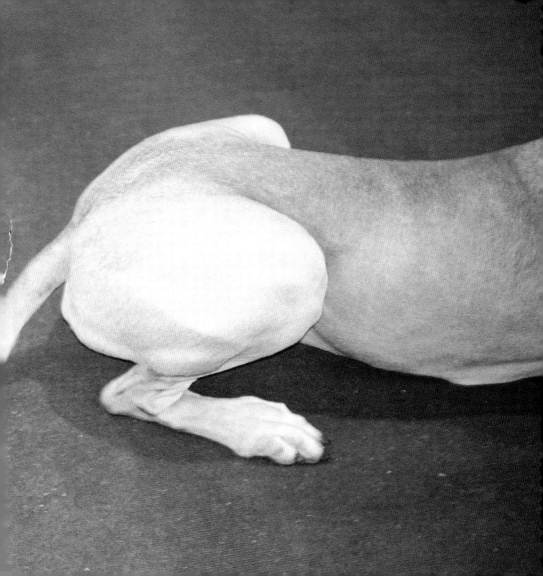